Copyright © Second Edition 2018 by White Horse LDS Books.

All rights reserved. Except as permitted under the United States Copyright Act of 1976, and in the case of brief quotations embodied in critical articles and reviews, no part of this publication may be copied, reproduced or distributed in any form or by any means, or stored in a database or retrieval system, without the prior written authorization from the author.

First Edition published October 2014
Second Edition published March 2018

**ISBN-13: 978-0-9904973-4-9**
**ISBN-10: 0990497348**
**BISAC: Religion**

Edited by Stephen R. Gorton
Artistic Cover Design by Connie Gorton

White Horse LDS Books
Salt Lake City, Utah 84108

# Hieroglyphs, Golden Plates And Typos

How Corrections in the Book of Mormon

Prove its Authenticity

## Bill Wylson

*Author's Note*: The principles discussed in this work relate to doctrines, procedures and practices of The Church of Jesus Christ of Latter-day Saints. I have attempted to cite sources from the scriptures and from the published writings of the General Authorities of the Church. Nevertheless, I have no authority or commission to speak in any official capacity for the Church. The ideas expressed herein represent nothing more than the opinion of the author.

Additionally, a testimony of the truthfulness of the Book of Mormon is founded on spiritual power. The primary assertion of the Book of Mormon, that Jesus is the Christ, the divine Son of God, is spiritual in nature. Things of the Spirit are known only through the power of the Spirit. You cannot gain a witness of a spiritual truth through physical evidence alone. While Heavenly Father will provide us with additional witnesses and proof that the statements of the Book of Mormon are true, such proof comes only *after* the exercise of faith. As Moroni stated; *"I . . . would show unto the world that faith is things which are hoped for and not seen; wherefore, dispute not because ye see not, for ye receive no witness until after the trial of your faith."* [1]

Bill Wylson

---

[1] Ether 12:6.

Praise for
# Hieroglyphs, Golden Plates and Typos

"Hieroglyphics, Golden Plates and Typos has a single, narrowly defined purpose: to draw attention to errors in the Book of Mormon. These errors, however, ... are presented as evidences that the book is precisely what it claims to be: an ancient text originally inscribed upon metal plates over the course of centuries by a number of historians. The study, ... is interesting, complete, and—for me at least—convincing."

*Michael*


"This was a great, brief read that brought out some interesting points about the reality of inscribing sacred records onto metal plates. Worth spending a couple of hours pondering..."

*Michael B.*


"Just finished reading Hieroglyphs, Golden Plates and Typos and really enjoyed this brief volume....

Don't be fooled by any part of the title, the mistakes help to prove that the Book of Mormon is the Word of God."

*Mark F.*

"Hieroglyphs, Golden Plates and Typos presents excellent evidence of the claims that the Book of Mormon is an ancient writing inscribed on metal plates which was later translated by the Prophet Joseph Smith. Wylson convincingly demonstrates how the original authors of the Book of Mormon corrected any "typos" or "slips of the stylus," as he calls them, and presents them as evidence of the origin of the Book of Mormon. A very interesting and faith-building book."

*Will H.*

"I really enjoyed learning about the history of The Book of Mormon. So often we talk about what is written and seldom think about the way the plates were made. This book was a refreshing perspective that now helps me see and think new things as I read the scriptures."

*Mike H.*

"Very informational."

*Kevin*

"I have been a Latter-day Saint for almost 43 years now, and I have lost count of the number of times I have read The Book of Mormon. This book gives me new insight. From now on, I can read The Book of Mormon with more understanding."

*K.C.*

# Table of Contents

The Most Correct Book ........................................................ - 15 -

The Problem with Plates ..................................................... - 19 -

Handling Hieroglyphics ...................................................... - 45 -

Slips of the Stylus ............................................................... - 61 -

Interpreting Typos .............................................................. - 69 -

Breakdown of Error Correction Frequency ....................... - 86 -

The Message in the Mistakes ............................................. - 89 -

The Only Absolute Proof .................................................... - 93 -

A Free Offer ...................................................................... - 101 -

About the Author ............................................................. - 105 -

Affectionately dedicated to my father, whose love of the scriptures and devotion to the Savior was an inspiration to thousands of people throughout the world but most emphatically within the walls of his own home.

*"We believe the Book of Mormon to be the word of God. God has so declared it, so have its writers, so have its witnesses, and so do all those who have read it and received a personal revelation from God as to its truthfulness."* – Ezra Taft Benson

## The Most Correct Book

On the inside cover of his first leather-bound Book of Mormon my father had written the following quotation from the prophet Joseph Smith;

*"I told the brethren that the Book of Mormon was the most correct of any book on earth, and the keystone of our religion, and a man would get nearer to God by abiding by its precepts, than by any other book."* [2]

Directly below this quote, my father had compiled a list of scriptures which he had labeled, "Mistakes in the Book of Mormon."

---

[2] Smith, Joseph, History of The Church of Jesus Christ of Latter-day Saints, vol. 4, p.461.

"Wait a minute," I hear you say. "The Book of Mormon is the word of God. It can't have 'mistakes' in it. Besides, didn't you just quote the Prophet Joseph Smith testifying that the Book of Mormon is 'the most correct of **any** book on earth?'"

I did and it is. The Book of Mormon was prepared by the Lord's prophets over a period of more than a thousand years. It was concealed by Moroni so that it would be preserved in its purity for future generations. Nothing testifies with more certainty of the magnitude of this modern-day book of scripture than the voice of the Savoir Himself!

In his book, *A Witness and a Warning*, [3] President Ezra Taft Benson delineates the Lord's own witness that;

- *The Book of Mormon is true,* [4]
- *It contains the word of God,* [5]
- *It was translated by power from on high,* [6]

---

[3] Benson, Ezra Taft, A Witness and a Warning, Deseret Book, Salt Lake City, Utah, 1988, p. 15.
[4] D&C 17:6.
[5] D&C 19:26.
[6] D&C 20:8.

- *It contains the fullness of the gospel of Jesus Christ,* [7]
- *It was given by inspiration and confirmed by the ministering of angels,* [8]
- *It gives evidence that the holy scriptures are true,* [9]
- *And those who receive it in faith shall receive eternal life.* [10]

After the death of his father, Moroni became custodian of the sacred archives. He then added what he thought would be the final two chapters to his father Mormon's account. He obviously did not expect to be writing anything further because, as he stated;

*"And behold, I would write* [the intent of the record] *also if I had room upon the plates, but I have not, and ore I have none, for I am alone."* [11]

Then, committing the writings to the future reader, Moroni candidly and apologetically acknowledged;

---

[7] D&C 20:9, 42:12.
[8] D&C 20:10.
[9] D&C 20:11.
[10] D&C 20:14.
[11] Mormon 8:5.

> *"And if there be faults they be the faults of a man. But behold, we know no fault."* [12]

How then did my father have the boldness to make his list of mistakes in the Book of Mormon? To gain a better understanding of the corrections in the Book of Mormon and how they testify to its truthfulness and authenticity, we need to understand the process involved in making plates of ore and the method for inscribing on them.

---

[12] Mormon 8:17.

## The Problem with Plates

I must confess, at times I become a little impatient with my computer. I sit down to write, press the power button and listen to the tower begin to whir. A power light illuminates at the base of the monitor, then, as the screen begins to glow, that familiar little circle starts turning on the display. Soon my desktop background appears and I enter my passcode. Again, the tower begins to whir and the little circle turns some more. When my home screen finally appears, I select my word processor, then find and select the document I want to work on. At long last, I am ready to begin writing.

Someone once told me; "Never complain about how slow your computer is. Just remember how things used to be."

I remember. My first typewriter was the manual kind, with a ribbon and a carriage that rang a bell when you reached the end of a line. I eventually graduated to an electric typewriter with a built in correction ribbon. As tough as those times seem to us now, they were nothing compared to the daunting task of writing a book on plates made from ore.

Think about what Nephi, Mormon, Moroni or any of the other ancient prophets had to go through just to have something permanent to write on!

The first challenge was finding the ore to molten into metal plates. Nephi obviously was not an expert at this since he had to go to the Lord for help. When the Lord instructed him to build a ship, Nephi asked the Lord;

"Whither shall I go that I may find ore to molten, that I may make tools to construct the ship?" [13]

I imagine the same would have been true for all the prophets who sought to record messages on metal plates. Imagine having to go out into a wilderness area and mine for metal before being able to write! Without the help of dynamite, rock drills,

---
[13] 1 Nephi 17:9.

jackhammers or any of our modern tools used for mining ore, these prophets had to excavate, gather and haul the ore to a place where it could be worked.

Once these writers of ancient scripture mined the ore from the ground, they then had to make a bellows, build a fire and molten the ore into useable materials. As Nephi explains;

*"I, Nephi, did make a bellows wherewith to blow the fire, of the skins of beasts;"* (which would have also involved hunting in the wilderness to obtain the skins) *"and after I had made a bellows…I did smite two stones together that I might make fire."* [14]

Having then smelted the ore, it is very probable that the metal was hammered or beaten, not cast, into the shape of plates, as seems to have been the practice in Israel.

*"And they did beat the gold into thin plates."* [15]

The plates that Joseph Smith unearthed on the hill Cumorah had been personally made by the

---

[14] 1 Nephi 17:11.
[15] Exodus 39:3.

hand of Mormon, and were called the Plates of Mormon. Mormon himself wrote;

*"I do make the record on plates which I have made with mine own hands."* [16]

All this work had to be performed before the prophets even began to write down their thoughts and record the words of God for future generations.

The Plates of Mormon that the prophet Joseph Smith uncovered contained the following sets of plates;

- A summation of Lehi's history known as the Large Plates of Nephi,
- The unabridged Small Plates made by Nephi and his successors,
- An abridgment of the record of the Jaredites made by Moroni,
- The writings of Moroni,
- And the sealed portion that was not translated by Joseph Smith.

These skillfully hand-made Plates of Mormon were about 6 x 8 x 6 inches and had the appearance of gold leaves that were not quite as thick as common

---

[16] 3 Nephi 5:11.

tin. They were engraved in reformed Egyptian and contained even less than a hundredth part of the history of Lehi and his family. These are the plates from which Joseph Smith translated the Book of Mormon by the gift and power of God before they were returned to the angel Moroni.

While he was in the process of translating the plates, Joseph Smith learned that many other records had been kept and preserved by Lehi's descendants. The history and doctrine from these other writings interweave through various chapters of the Book of Mormon. They combine to make a complementing witness of the Savior and His divine mission.

Elder Boyd K. Packer said;

*"As the influence of that message is traced from generation to generation, more than twenty writers record the fate of individuals and of civilizations who accepted or rejected that testament."* [17]

---

[17] Packer, Boyd K., Ensign, April 1986, p. 74.

Lehi carried with him the plates of Laban, scriptures recorded on brass plates, as he and his family journeyed toward the Promised Land.

Nephi wrote;

*"And behold, it is wisdom in God that we should obtain these records, that we may preserve unto our children the language of our fathers;*

*"And also that we may preserve unto them the words which have been spoken by the mouth of all the holy prophets, which have been delivered unto them by the Spirit and power of God, since the world began, even down unto this present time."* [18]

The Brass Plates of Laban contained;

- The five books of Moses, detailing the creation of the world, and the account of our first parents, Adam and Eve; [19]
- A record of the Jews from the beginning, down to the commencement of the reign of Zedekiah, king of Judah; [20]

---

[18] 1 Ne. 3:19, 20.
[19] 1 Ne. 5:11.
[20] 1 Ne. 5:12.

- The words of all the holy prophets, delivered to them by the spirit and power of God; [21]
- And a genealogy of Lehi's ancestors. [22]

Similar in content but much more complete than our present day Old Testament [23] (up until the time Lehi left Jerusalem), the Brass Plates were extremely important to Lehi's family. Not only did they preserve the people's language but they also safeguarded their spiritual heritage.

About 130 B.C., King Benjamin explained to his sons that...

*"...were it not for these plates, which contain these records and these commandments, we must have suffered in ignorance, even at this present time, not knowing the mysteries of God."* [24]

Alma later explained to his son Helaman that the Brass Plates...

*"...have enlarged the memory of this people, yea, and convinced many of the error of their ways,*

---

[21] 1 Ne. 5:13 (see also 1 Ne. 3:20).
[22] 1 Ne. 5 14.
[23] 1 Nephi 13:23.
[24] Mosiah 1:3.

*and brought them to the knowledge of their God unto the salvation of their souls."* [25]

Mormon did not abridge the Brass Plates of Laban nor did he include them in his record. He did include verses and chapters from them which support and clarify many Biblical doctrines. The Brass Plates established the pattern for the Nephite practice of writing on metal plates and determined the language used in their sacred writings.

After leaving Jerusalem, Lehi began keeping a separate record of his own which would ultimately form the basis of a major portion of the Book of Mormon.

As Boyd K. Packer further explains;

*"He kept something of a secular account of their journeys, interspersed with his revelations and teachings and spiritual experiences. Nephi succeeded his father, Lehi, as keeper of the record, which became known as the large plates of Nephi."* [26]

Nephi explained that on the Large Plates...

---

[25] Alma 37:8.
[26] Packer, Boyd K., Ensign, May 1986, p. 59.

"...should be engraven an account of the reign of the kings, and the wars and contentions of my people." [27]

He also described his intent in recording the Large Plates;

"And it came to pass that the Lord commanded me, wherefore I did make plates of ore that I might engraven upon them the record of my people. And upon the plates which I made I did engraven the record of my father, and also our journeyings in the wilderness, and the prophecies of my father; and also many of mine own prophecies have I engraven upon them.

"Wherefore, I, Nephi, did make a record upon the other plates, which gives an account, or which gives a greater account of the wars and contentions and destructions of my people. And this have I done, and commanded my people what they should do after I was gone; and that these plates should be handed down from one generation to another." [28]

---

[27] 1 Nephi 9:4.
[28] 1 Nephi 19:1, 4.

The Large Plates became the historical record of Nephi and his descendants. They include a large and thorough account of the people of Nephi in the Promised Land. Then, according to Nephi's instructions, these plates were expanded and handed down from generation to generation.

Jarom, the son of Enos and grandson of Nephi's younger brother Jacob, explained that;

*"Ye can go to the other plates of Nephi; for behold, upon them the records of our wars are engraven, according to the writings of the kings, or those which they caused to be written."* [29]

For roughly four hundred years these Large Plates were principally historical, recorded and kept by the rulers up until the time of King Benjamin, (about 130 B.C.), when apparently they became the responsibility of the prophets.

Nephi, however, had been commanded to make a second record for a *"wise purpose"*. [30]

The Lord told Nephi;

---

[29] Jarom 1:14.
[30] 1 Nephi 9:5.

"Make other plates; and thou shalt engraven many things upon them which are good in my sight, for the profit of thy people." [31]

These *"other plates"* were to become known as the Small Plates of Nephi.

"Wherefore, I, Nephi, to be obedient to the commandments of the Lord, went and made these plates upon which I have engraven these things.

"And I engraved that which is pleasing unto God. And if my people are pleased with the things of God they will be pleased with mine engravings which are upon these plates.

"And if my people desire to know the more particular part of the history of my people they must search mine other plates." [32]

He further explains;

"And upon these I write the things of my soul, and many of the scriptures which are engraven upon the plates of brass. For my soul delighteth in the scriptures, and my heart pondereth them, and

---

[31] 2 Nephi 5:30.
[32] 2 Nephi 5:31-33.

writeth them for the learning and profit of my children." ³³

Jacob also described the intent of these Small Plates;

"And he gave me, Jacob, a commandment that I should write upon these plates a few of the things which I considered to be most precious; that I should not touch, save it were lightly, concerning the history of this people which are called the people of Nephi.

"For he said that the history of his people should be engraven upon his other plates, and that I should preserve these plates and hand them down unto my seed, from generation to generation.

"And if there were preaching which was sacred, or revelation which was great, or prophesying, that I should engraven the heads of them upon these plates, and touch upon them as much as it were possible, for Christ's sake, and for the sake of our people." ³⁴

---

[33] 2 Nephi 4:15.
[34] Jacob 1:2-4.

The Large Plates of Nephi, then, were kept and expanded by the kings but the small plates were kept by the prophets. Nephi wrote;

*"I have received a commandment of the Lord that I should make these plates, for the special purpose that there should be an account engraven of the ministry of my people."* [35]

*"It mattereth not to me that I am particular to give a full account of all the things of my father, for they cannot be written upon these plates, for I desire the room that I may write of the things of God.*

*"For the fulness of mine intent is that I may persuade men to come unto the God of Abraham, and the God of Isaac, and the God of Jacob, and be saved.*

*"Wherefore, I shall give commandment unto my seed, that they shall not occupy these plates with things which are not of worth unto the children of men."* [36]

---

[35] 1 Nephi 9:3.
[36] 1 Nephi 6:3-4, 6.

"And this I do that the more sacred things may be kept for the knowledge of my people. Nevertheless, I do not write anything upon plates save it be that I think it be sacred." [37]

Nephi entrusted the Small Plates to his younger brother, Jacob, who later delivered them to his son, Enos. Then Jarom, Omni, Amaron, Chemish, Abinadom and Amaleki, and each in turn kept the records. When finally no room remained on the Small Plates that Nephi had made, Amaleki, the last prophet to write on them, comes to the end of the last plate with the abrupt pronouncement that...

"...these plates are full. And I make an end of my speaking." [38]

With no more room remaining on the Small Plates of Nephi, they were turned over to King Benjamin [39] for safekeeping. From that time on the Small Plates were kept unaltered and the Large Plates of Nephi were used to record both secular and spiritual events. Since there was no longer a separate spiritual record, all of the teachings, visions, and

---

[37] 1 Nephi 19:5-6.
[38] Omni 1:30.
[39] Omni 1:25.

prophecies of the Nephites were recorded along with their history on the Large Plates.

Combining the secular and religious records produced a more balanced account. All of the records of Nephi were kept by righteous men, most of whom were prophets, political heads or military leaders. And so it continued until about the year A.D. 320, when the prophet Ammaron...

*"...being constrained by the Holy Ghost, did hide up the records which were sacred—yea, even all the sacred records which had been handed down from generation to generation."* [40]

Mormon then explains;

*"And about the time that Ammaron hid up the records unto the Lord, he came unto me, (I being about ten years of age, and I began to be learned somewhat after the manner of the learning of my people) and Ammaron said unto me: I perceive that thou art a sober child, and art quick to observe;*

*"Therefore, when ye are about twenty and four years old I would that ye should remember the things that ye have observed concerning this*

---

[40] 4 Nephi 1:48.

people; and when ye are of that age go to the land Antum, unto a hill which shall be called Shim; and there have I deposited unto the Lord all the sacred engravings concerning this people.

"And behold, ye shall take the plates of Nephi unto yourself, and the remainder shall ye leave in the place where they are; and ye shall engrave on the plates of Nephi all the things that ye have observed concerning this people." [41]

Mormon remembered and obeyed Ammaron's directives. When he received the plates that Ammaron had concealed, he added to the Large Plates of Nephi a *"full account"* [42] of his people and the events that occurred during his life.

"And behold I had gone according to the word of Ammaron, and taken the plates of Nephi, and did make a record according to the words of Ammaron.

"And upon the plates of Nephi I did make a full account of all the wickedness and abominations." [43]

---

[41] Mormon 1:2-4.
[42] Mormon 2:18.
[43] Mormon 2:17-18.

He later abridged this record for the latter-day account.[44] Years later, Mormon was instructed to make a smaller record of his people, an abridgment of the larger records. He wrote;

*"And it hath become expedient that I, according to the will of God, that the prayers of those who have gone hence, who were the holy ones, should be fulfilled according to their faith, should make a record of these things which have been done—*

*"Yea, a small record of that which hath taken place from the time that Lehi left Jerusalem, even down until the present time.*

*"Therefore I do make my record from the accounts which have been given by those who were before me, until the commencement of my day."* [45]

*"Therefore I write a small abridgment, daring not to give a full account of the things which I have seen."* [46]

Mormon included in his record the unabridged Small Plates of Nephi. In a final attempt

---

[44] Ibid.
[45] 3 Nephi 5:14-16.
[46] Mormon 5:9.

to preserve the records and their sacred teachings, Mormon hid them all in the hill Cumorah. He gave only a few of the plates to his son Moroni.

*"I, Mormon, began to be old; and knowing it to be the last struggle of my people, and having been commanded of the Lord that I should not suffer the records which had been handed down by our fathers, which were sacred, to fall into the hands of the Lamanites, (for the Lamanites would destroy them) therefore I made this record out of the plates of Nephi, and hid up in the hill Cumorah all the records which had been entrusted to me by the hand of the Lord, save it were these few plates which I gave unto my son Moroni."* [47]

Near the end of his life, Mormon wrote a letter to his son.

*"I trust that I may see thee soon; for I have sacred records that I would deliver up unto thee."* [48]

Mormon's desire was granted. He was able to preserve all the sacred records of his people and give

---

[47] Mormon 6:6.
[48] Mormon 9:24.

*"these few plates"* [49] to Moroni, who then completed the record and hid up the plates.

It would appear that the Plates of Mormon which Moroni received were small and almost full. Not long after the destruction of his people in 385 A.D., Moroni writes;

*"Behold I, Moroni, do finish the record of my father, Mormon. Behold, I have but few things to write, which things I have been commanded by my father.*

*"And my father also was killed by them, and I even remain alone to write the sad tale of the destruction of my people. But behold, they are gone, and I fulfil the commandment of my father. And whether they will slay me, I know not.*

*"Behold, my father hath made this record, and he hath written the intent thereof. And behold, I would write it also if I had room upon the plates, but I have not; and ore I have none, for I am alone. My father hath been slain in battle, and all my kinsfolk, and I have not friends nor whither to go;*

---

[49] Mormon 6:6.

and how long the Lord will suffer that I may live I know not."⁵⁰

Some fifteen years later, in 400 A.D., Moroni came back to the plates, added eight more verses and closed his account by saying;

"And whoso receiveth this record, and shall not condemn it because of the imperfections which are in it, the same shall know of greater things than these. Behold, I am Moroni; and were it possible, I would make all things known unto you.

"Behold, I make an end of speaking concerning this people. I am the son of Mormon, and my father was a descendant of Nephi." ⁵¹

And so, after fifteen years of living alone and hiding out from the Lamanites, Moroni still had no additional plates to write on. His closing comments were brief as he bid farewell to his future readers.

Then something changed. The third time Moroni returned for the plates, room for writing was no longer a problem. Moroni finished the record of his father, abridged the twenty-four Gold Plates of

---

⁵⁰ Mormon 8:1, 3, 5.
⁵¹ Mormon 8:12-13.

Ether, wrote his own book, wrote part of the title page, and added a large amount which was sealed and not translated by Joseph Smith.

The twenty-four Plates of Ether which Moroni abridged when he again had plates to write on contained the record of the Jaredites, found by the people of Limhi in the days of King Mosiah. Moroni began this abridgment, stating;

*"And now I, Moroni, proceed to give an account of those ancient inhabitants who were destroyed by the hand of the Lord upon the face of this north country.*

*"And I take mine account from the twenty and four plates which were found by the people of Limhi, which is called the Book of Ether."* [52]

The Jaredites were a separate people from the family of Lehi. They came to the Promised Land a short time after the languages were confounded at the Tower of Babel. Their records were translated with the help of "interpreters" prepared by the Lord for that very purpose. Ether, the last prophet of the Jaredites, was rejected by his people, and, while

---

[52] Ether 1:1-2.

hiding in caves, recorded the complete destruction of the Jaredite nation. [53]

Moroni recorded in grand detail the visions and teachings of the brother of Jared. He said;

*"Behold, I have written upon these plates the very things which the brother of Jared saw; and there never were greater things made manifest than those which were made manifest unto the brother of Jared.*

*"Wherefore the Lord hath commanded me to write them; and I have written them. And he commanded me that I should seal them up."* [54]

So Moroni sealed this portion of the plates and included in his writings a warning to the future translator;

*"And I have told you the things which I have sealed up; therefore touch them not in order that ye may translate; for that thing is forbidden you, except by and by it shall be wisdom in God."* [55]

---

[53] Ether 13:13, 14.
[54] Ether 4:4, 5 (see also 2 Ne. 27:7).
[55] Ether 5:1.

Estimates on how large a portion of the Plates of Mormon were sealed range from one-third to two-thirds. However, the prophet Joseph Smith simply stated; "*a part of which was sealed.*" [56] Whatever the actual amount may be, Moroni's sealed plates are extensive and extremely valuable and will one day be made available to us.

Elder Bruce R. McConkie commented on the contents of these sealed writings;

*"When, during the Millennium, the sealed portion of the Book of Mormon is translated, it will give an account of life in the premortal existence; of the creation of all things; of the Fall and the Atonement and the Second Coming; of temple ordinances, in their fulness; of the ministry and mission of translated beings; of life in the spirit world, in both paradise and hell; of the kingdoms of glory to be inhabited by resurrected beings; and many such like things.*

*"As of now, the world is not ready to receive these truths."* [57]

---

[56] HC 4:537.
[57] McConkie, Bruce R., "The Bible, a Sealed Book," address given at CES Symposium, August 1984, p. 1.

In 421 A.D., Moroni ended his writing and buried the Plates of Mormon where they remained until he personally delivered them to Joseph Smith in 1827. These then are what are known as the Plates of Mormon and are the plates from which Joseph translated the Book of Mormon.

For over a thousand years, the Lord had developed the background resources from which He would compose the most influential witness of Jesus Christ ever written, together with the visions and writings of numerous prophets, the histories of nations; their blessings and covenants, their disobedience and eventual destruction.

A lifetime of obedience and service had prepared Mormon to compile what would become known as *The Book of Mormon, Another Testament of Jesus Christ*. At the Lord's command Mormon began his labor of love…

*"…to come forth by the gift and power of God….to the convincing of the Jew and Gentile that Jesus is the Christ, the eternal God."* [58]

The Book of Mormon, published in March 1830, made available to the world the sacred plates

---

[58] Book of Mormon, title page.

chosen by the Lord to stand as a witness of Jesus Christ. These plates contain the following promise to those who believe the Book of Mormon;

*"Then shall the greater things be made manifest unto them."* [59]

And for those who do not believe it;

*"Then shall the greater things be withheld from them, unto their condemnation."* [60]

---

[59] 3 Nephi 26:9.
[60] 3 Nephi 26:10.

# Handling Hieroglyphics

The prophet Joseph Smith did not reveal very much about the nature of the characters with which the Book of Mormon was written, or the methods involved in its translation. The limited yet intriguing verses from the Book of Mormon detailing the subject actually raise more questions than they answer.

Nephi states at the beginning of his work that he made the record;

*"...in the language of my father, which consists of the learning of the Jews and the language of the Egyptians."* [61]

---

[61] 1 Nephi 1:2.

One theory states that Egyptian characters were used to convey the Hebrew language. As Book of Mormon scholar George Reynolds writes;

*"The words 'language of the Egyptians' very probably means little more than Egyptian characters or an alphabet for spelling Hebrew words."* [62]

This suggests that the Book of Mormon was written in Hebrew using Egyptian characters. The Book of Mormon, however, states very specifically that it was written in the *language* of the Egyptians and not simply using Egyptian characters. [63]

The *"learning of the Jews"* undoubtedly refers to the structure and style of the Hebrew language used in writing the Book of Mormon. It is, however, quite possible that Nephi was proposing an even more comprehensive notion of *"the learning of the Jews"* than just their style of writing or speaking.

Nephi, commenting on the difficulty of comprehending the words of Isaiah, wrote that;

---

[62] Reynolds, George, The Story of the Book of Mormon, Zions Printing and Publication Co., Independence, 1915, p. 288.

[63] 1 Nephi 1:2; Mormon. 9:32-33.

*"Isaiah spake many things which were hard for many of my people to understand; for **they know not concerning the manner of prophesying among the Jews**. For I, Nephi, have not taught them many things concerning the manner of the Jews....And I know that the Jews do understand the things of the prophets, and there is none other people that understand the things which were spoken unto the Jews like unto them, **save it be that they are taught after the manner of the things of the Jews**."* [64]

Rather than a reference to the style and structure of their language, *"the learning of the Jews"* refers more fittingly to *"the manner of the Jews"* [65] and *"the manner of prophesying among the Jews."* [66]

Nephi explains;

*"I, Nephi, have not taught my children after the manner of the Jews."* [67]

Obviously, *"the learning of the Jews"* does not signify the structure of their language since

---

[64] 2 Nephi 25:1, 2, 5.
[65] 2 Nephi 25:2.
[66] 2 Nephi 25:1.
[67] 2 Nephi 25:6.

Nephi's children *were* taught in the language of the Jews. Hebrew remained the common language of both the Nephites and the Lamanites for over a thousand years.

Moroni stated that the Egyptian language was used to conserve room on the plates he engraved. A character expressing an idea would be much more concise than a phonetic character of the Hebrew alphabet.

Hieroglyphs (from the Greek *hieros* meaning sacred and *glypho* meaning sculpture) were generally reserved for sacred writings. Types of hieroglyphic writing include;

- Chinese characters,
- Egyptian hieroglyphs, and
- Iraqi cuneiforms.

They began as pictures representing objects from the real world. Then, as civilizations needed to communicate more abstract ideas, these *"pictograms"* were employed as symbols for the sounds of the items they represented. These were then called *"phonetograms"*.

In their most advanced form, hieroglyphs are made up of three distinct classes of symbols;

- pictograms,
- phonetograms, and
- determinatives.

Determinatives were used to assist the reader in discerning the meaning of a certain symbol.

The earliest Egyptian hieroglyphics date from about 3000 B.C. and remained in use until the Greco-Roman period when they became largely phonetic. Hieratic writing, a more cursive form of hieroglyphs, began around 2450 B.C. and was commonly found on papyrus until it, too, was replaced by the simplified, phonetic demotic script.[68]

A few Mormon scholars have suggested that the Book of Mormon was written in demotic characters since the demotic script was familiar in Lehi's time. The Book of Mormon, however, clearly states that Lehi understood the language of the Egyptians [69] and that both he and the Old Testament

---

[68] The Eerdmans Bible Dictionary, William B. Eerdmans Publishing Company, Grand Rapids, MI, 1987.
[69] Mosiah 1:3-4.

prophet Jeremiah [70] recorded their prophecies on the Brass Plates of Laban which were written in Egyptian.

Considering the difficulty in making metal plates, it became critical to conserve space on the records prepared by the Nephite authors. Writing in Egyptian hieroglyphs rather than in their native Hebrew allowed the writers to conserve space on the precious metal plates. Moroni wrote;

"We have written this record according to our knowledge, in the characters which are called among us the reformed Egyptian, being handed down and altered by us, according to our manner of speech. **And if our plates had been sufficiently large we should have written in Hebrew.**" [71]

Demotic Egyptian was phonetic, each character representing a unit of speech, therefore, there would have been no substantial space saving over writing in Hebrew. The Nephite prophets would have taken up *more* space on the plates writing in

---

[70] 1 Nephi 5:13.
[71] Mormon 9:32, 33.

demotic characters than writing in their native Hebrew.

The use of pictograms representing distinctive phonetic characters of speech in the Book of Mormon is unreasonable since it would have made the Book of Mormon longer instead of shorter than if written in Hebrew. This is evident in the Chinese translation of the Book of Mormon which employs a given Chinese character for each English syllable. While there are fewer Chinese characters than English letters in the Book of Mormon, the Chinese Book of Mormon is 718 pages long while the English version is only 531 pages long!

Saving enough space to warrant writing in a foreign language instead of the familiar Hebrew would require an ideogram form of writing. Consequently, the Book of Mormon was in all probability written with hieroglyphic or hieratic characters used principally as ideograms.

A similar comparison of this space saving technique is found in the Rosetta stone inscribed in 196 B.C. This artifact contains an engraving written in two idioms, Egyptian and Greek. The Egyptian inscription is written in hieroglyphics, then repeated in demotic characters. Translators believe that the text was first written in demotic, then re-written in hieroglyphics and translated into Greek before being transcribed onto the stone. [72]

A rough idea of the possible amount of space saved from Greek to demotic and from demotic to hieroglyphics can be determined by studying the number of characters and the amount of space used for each of these three scripts.

The demotic inscription comprises 23% less space than the Greek inscription. The text contains 54 lines of Greek writing and only 32 lines of demotic. The demotic text contains approximately 3360 characters. The Greek text contains about 6700 characters. The compression of demotic over Greek is about two to one.

Part of the hieroglyphic inscription on the Rosetta stone has been broken off, leaving only 14 lines of hieroglyphs intact. These 14 lines match the last 18 lines of the demotic writing and the last 28 lines of the Greek. The height of the hieroglyphs is about twice that of the demotic and three times that of the Greek characters.

---

[72] Andrews, Carol, The British Museum Book of the Rosetta Stone, Peter Bedrick Books, New York, 1985, p. 45.

If the hieroglyphs on the Rosetta were equal in size to the demotic, the text would have been half the size that it was. Then only seven lines of hieroglyphs would have corresponded to 18 lines of demotic. Consequently, in order to conserve the necessary space, the Book of Mormon authors must have used a highly pictographic, rather than phonetic, Egyptian writing.

Additionally, Joseph Smith reported that the characters on the Book of Mormon plates *"were small, and beautifully engraved."* [73]

Another Book of Mormon scholar, J. M. Sjodahl, acquired several pages of the English text of the Book of Mormon translated into contemporary Hebrew and another translated into the Israeli characters common in Lehi's day. The contemporary translation reduces the English by 14 to 1 but the ancient Hebrew reduces the English by 7 to 1. [74]

Since English and Greek are phonetically similar, the Israeli characters of Lehi's time would have taken up only one seventh the space of the Greek. In other words, the Israeli characters take up

---

[73] Smith, Joseph, The Wentworth Letter, March 1, 1842.
[74] Sjodahl, J. M., An Introduction to the Study of the Book of Mormon, Deseret News Press, Salt Lake City, 1927, p.39.

less than one-third the space of the demotic! So it appears highly unlikely that the Nephites would have written in demotic since there wasn't enough room on the plates to write in their own native Hebrew language.

If the Nephites inscribed their sacred records with early Egyptian hieroglyphs rather than demotic characters, the most likely source for those characters would have been the Brass Plates of Laban. They apparently included the Old Testament writings up to the time of Zedekiah, along with the writings of other prophets not mentioned in the Old Testament, such as Ezias, Neum, Zenock and Zenos. Nephi tells us that the Brass Plates contained;

*"...the five books of Moses, which gave an account of the creation of the world, and also of Adam and Eve, who were our first parents; And also a record of the Jews from the beginning, even down to the commencement of the reign of Zedekiah, king of Judah; And also the prophecies of the holy prophets, from the beginning, even down to the commencement of the reign of Zedekiah; and also many prophecies which have been spoken by the mouth of Jeremiah."* [75]

---

[75] 1 Nephi 5:11-13.

We also know that both Lehi and Jeremiah wrote their prophecies on the Brass Plates in the Egyptian language.

The Brass Plates of Laban were likely an original document and carried the accounts written by each of the prophets and kings whose works appear in the record, in the same manner as the writings of the Nephite prophets and kings were added to the Large Plates of Nephi. [76]

When the Lord called Moses to lead the children of Israel out of the land of Egypt, Moses protested, saying;

*"O my Lord, I am not eloquent, neither heretofore, nor since thou has spoken unto thy servant: but I am slow of speech, and of a slow tongue."* [77]

So the Lord appointed Aaron, his brother, to be a spokesman for him. Some people have erroneously interpreted this passage to mean that Moses had a speech impediment. Such was not the

---

[76] Gorton, H. Clay, The Legacy of the Brass Plates of Laban, Horizon Publishers, Bountiful, Utah, 1994, p.14-22.
[77] Exodus 4:10.

case. Relating the history of Israel before the Sanhedrin, Stephen stated that;

*"Moses was learned in all the wisdom of the Egyptians,* **and was mighty in words** *and in deeds."* [78]

When Moses said he was *"slow of speech,"* he only meant that he had difficulty speaking in the Hebrew language.

Moses was raised as an Egyptian in the court of Pharaoh. When Moses visited the Jews in the land of Goshen, they considered him an Egyptian and not one of their own. Moses later fled Egypt after killing another Egyptian for wrongfully oppressing one of the Hebrew slaves. For forty years Moses lived with his father-in-law Jethro, a Midianite. The Midianites were a confederation of Arab tribes. Moses most likely didn't even begin speaking the Hebrew language until his 40-year sojourn with the children of Israel in the desert.

As Moses recorded the first five books of the Old Testament, detailing the account of the creation, God's interactions with his children from Adam to

---

[78] Acts 7:22.

Abraham, the exodus from Egypt and the Mosaic Law given on Mount Sanai, it would only make sense that he would document his writings on material that would endure the test of time, such as brass plates, and serve as a benefit for later generations. Considering that he was not eloquent in Hebrew but educated in the wisdom of the Egyptians and mighty in words in his native Egyptian language, certainly he would have written his account in Egyptian.

Ancient Egyptians believed that written symbols had special powers. They reserved the more stylish hieroglyphs for religious writings. Hieratic symbols were more practical and were used primarily for economic, literary and scientific writings. Composing such a significant and sacred religious record as the Pentateuch, Moses would have undoubtedly adhered to the customs of the Egyptians and written with hieroglyphs instead of hieratic characters.

Moses' successors would need to learn to read Egyptian hieroglyphs to be able interpret the holy writings and the laws given to them on Mount Sanai. It is very likely then that the ensuing prophets and kings recorded their histories and prophecies in hieroglyphs also. It seems reasonable that the Brass Plates of Laban would have been the original scriptures recorded by each of the prophets and kings beginning with Moses down to the time of the prophets Lehi and Jeremiah.

This being the case, it would have been necessary for Lehi to be fluent in Egyptian in order to be able to read the Brass Plates. Nephi not only wrote...

*"...in the language of my father, which consists of... the language of the Egyptians..."* [79]

But Lehi himself was...

*"...taught in all the language of the Egyptians."* [80]

The Egyptian that Lehi and the subsequent Book of Mormon authors were taught was the ancient hieroglyphs of the Brass Plates of Laban. If the Book of Mormon authors had been taught and had written in the demotic language of the Egyptians, it would not have saved any space on the plates. Writing their sacred religious records in Egyptian hieroglyphs may have been as much a habit from their history with the Brass Plates as it was a necessity for saving space on the Plates of Nephi and

---

[79] 1 Nephi 1:2.
[80] Mosiah 1:4.

the abridgements made by Mormon and his son, Moroni.

# Slips of the Stylus

Whenever I made a mistake typing on my old manual typewriter, it usually meant that I had to throw an entire sheet away and begin typing all over again. I certainly fit the iconic comic image of the man slumped over his typewriter, the wastebasket next to him overflowing with crumpled sheets of paper. When preparing a manuscript for publication, typos and white-out were considered unacceptable. My electric typewriter had a self-correcting ribbon and I could hide a few minor mistakes if I caught them in time. But even then, if I had typed too far into the document, I still would have had to start over.

The great advantage to writing with a state-of-the-art word processor is that many of my typos are auto-corrected on the screen before I even see them. (For instance, just try misspelling *"recieve"* and see what happens.) The misspelled words that are not auto-corrected show up on the screen with a red line beneath them, reminiscent of the big red circles my grade school teacher drew around any misspelled words in my school assignments. Other mistakes, like typing 'deer' when I meant to type 'dear' slip by the spell check program altogether.

But even with all of these programs and safeguards, I still tend to find mistakes that escape detection. After I have done everything I can to correct my errors, it is then up to my editor to catch the mistakes I missed and see that they are corrected.

Moroni had none of these advantages at his disposal. He spent his days, months and years, alone and in hiding, scrawling out his message to future generations on gold plates made with his own hand. Under the weight of this heavy task, Moroni may have felt somewhat uncertain and insecure in his abilities, especially while working on the translation of the Jaredite record. The Jaredite plates were written in a pure language that had not been confounded at the tower of Babel. It must have been extremely frustrating for Moroni to translate from the pure Jaredite language into a reformed version of the Egyptian language, which was not even his native tongue but a language that was essentially foreign to him.

He addressed his concerns with the Lord, saying;

"...Lord, the gentiles will mock at these things because of our weakness in writing, for Lord, thou hast made us mighty in word by faith but thou hast not made us mighty in writing." [81]

We have seen that Moroni's concern that *"if there be faults they be the faults of a man"* [82] arose from the fact that the Book of Mormon plates were inscribed with the hieroglyphs of a reformed Egyptian writing, rather than with the modified Hebrew commonly spoken by the Nephites.

We now know that the Egyptian language was used to save space on the sacred records since a pictogram illustrating an idea is much more succinct than phonetic characters representing the elemental sounds of speech. As Moroni states;

"And now, behold, we have written this record according to our knowledge, in the

---

[81] Ether 12:23.
[82] Mormon 8:17.

*characters which are called among us the reformed Egyptian, being handed down and altered by us, according to our manner of speech. And if our plates had been sufficiently large we should have written in Hebrew, but the Hebrew hath been altered by us also; and if we could have written in Hebrew, behold, ye would have had no imperfection in our record."* [83]

Moroni's allusion to potential faults and imperfections in the Book of Mormon is very significant and even intriguing. The very nature of these "imperfections" testify to the truthfulness and authenticity of these sacred writings known today as The Book of Mormon.

It's happened to all of us; you sit down to write a letter to a friend, or copy a recipe onto a card, or perhaps to write a paper for work or school. You begin writing and suddenly notice a mistake you've made. Maybe your mind got ahead of your pen and you left out a word, or maybe you simply misspelled something. This is a common fault we have all experienced at one time or another. In our world it's no big deal, since a mistake can easily be deleted, erased, whited-out, backspaced over or even wadded up and re-written. As we are about to discover, it was

---

[83] Mormon 9:32, 33.

much more problematic for the ancient prophets and kings etching foreign-language hieroglyphs into thin sheets of metal.

Inscribing hieroglyphs onto these thin sheets of metal was not an easy undertaking. Jacob stated;

*"I cannot write but a little of my words, because of the difficulty of engraving our words upon plates and we know that the things which we write upon plates must remain...*

*"...and we labor diligently to engraven these words upon plates."* [84]

Despite their diligent labors, these ancient scribes were human, just like us, with all the potential for making human mistakes that we suffer from. Undoubtedly inscribing with some sort of stylus, the Book of Mormon authors would, from time to time, accidentally write an unintended word or phrase. Several of these "stylographical" errors occurred as the writers recorded their thoughts on the golden plates.

With the enormous amount of work involved in making thin metal sheets to write on, these

---

[84] Jacob 4:1-3.

prophets couldn't just crumple up their writing, toss it in the waste basket and start over as we so often do. They could, of course, simply scratch out the mistake but then the elegance and purity of their painstaking labor would be lost and the forthcoming translator of the writings would have to determine if the scratch marks were actually part of the hieroglyph!

All of the Book of Mormon writers were sensitive to the sacred nature of the significant record they were preparing for future generations. They were also aware that we would not know or understand their language. Nephi saw in vision the recipients of his writings. Directing his words to the future readers of the Plates of Nephi, he concludes his account with the statement;

*"And now, my beloved brethren, and also Jew, and all ye ends of the earth, hearken unto these words and believe in Christ... And now, my beloved brethren, all those who are of the house of Israel, and all ye ends of the earth, I speak unto you as the voice of one crying from the dust."* [85]

Moroni reveals as he finishes his father's writings that he saw our day in vision. He describes

---

[85] 2 Nephi 33:10-13.

the societal setting that would exist when the Book of Mormon came out of darkness into light, [86] stating;

*"The Lord hath shown unto me great and marvelous things concerning that which must shortly come, at that day when these things shall come forth among you.*

*"Behold, I speak unto you as if ye were present, and yet ye are not. But behold, Jesus Christ hath shown you unto me, and I know your doing."*[87]

He also asserts;

*"Behold, I speak unto you as though I spake from the dead; for I know that ye shall have my words."* [88]

Surely all of the contributing authors of the Book of Mormon also sensed that their record would be of immeasurable worth to future generations. Knowing that their language would disappear, Moroni placed the Urim and Thummim, or

---

[86] See Mormon 8:26-33.
[87] Mormon 8:34, 35.
[88] Mormon 9:30.

interpreters, with the plates to facilitate in their translation. [89]

With such a sacred assignment it is certain that the Book of Mormon authors were concerned, not only with the message contained on the plates, but also, with how their words were inscribed.

---

[89] Ether 4:5.

## Interpreting Typos

So what do you do when you inadvertently make a mistake while inscribing foreign hieroglyphs onto gold plates? You can't really start over and you don't want to mar the plates by scratching out the character. The Book of Mormon authors developed and used a more practical and ingenious method of correction whenever such errors occurred. The writer would remedy the mistake using the conjunction *"or"*, and then re-writing his words in proper form.

Four functions of the conjunction *"or"* are widely used throughout the Book of Mormon...

- To show opposites,
- To show equivalents,
- To paraphrase, and
- To correct.

To better interpret how the inspired authors of the Book of Mormon employed the corrective "or" conjunction, we need to first look at these four distinct uses of the word "or."

The following two verses illustrate how the exclusive form of *"or"* is used to show opposites;

*"And they are free **to choose liberty and eternal life**, through the great Mediator of all men, **or to choose captivity and death** according to the captivity and power of the devil."*[90]

*"Yea, and I know that good and evil have come before all men; he that knoweth not good from evil is blameless; but he that knoweth good and evil, to him it is given according to his desires, whether he desireth **good or evil, life or death, joy or remorse of conscience.**"* [91]

The above verses demonstrate how the word "or" is used in comparisons, this *or* that, one *or* the other.

The exclusive form of *"or"* is also used to show equivalents, as in these next two passages;

---

[90] 2 Nephi 2:27.
[91] Alma 29:5.

"And thus, in their prosperous circumstances, they did not send away any who were **naked** or that were **hungry** or that were **athirst** or that were **sick**, or that had **not been nourished**." [92]

"Yea, after having been such a highly favored people of the Lord; yea, after having been favored above every other **nation, kindred, tongue** or **people**." [93]

The next three verses illustrate how the word "or" is used in paraphrasing;

"Behold, I have **dreamed a dream** or, in other words, I have **seen a vision**." [94]

"Hearken and hear this, O house of Jacob, who are called by the name of Israel, and are come forth **out of the waters of Judah**, or **out of the waters of baptism**." [95]

"...and also the **ball**, or **compass**." [96]

---

[92] Alma 1:30.
[93] Alma 9:20.
[94] 1 Nephi 8:2.
[95] 1 Nephi 20:1.
[96] 2 Nephi 5:12.

The above uses of the word "or" are common and widely used in all writing today. To uncover the human imperfections and faults of the Book of Mormon writers and to reveal the significance of their distinct method of correcting errors, we need to examine the specific "corrective" use of the word "*or*".

The corrective *"or" is* unique to the Book of Mormon, no doubt owing to the way in which it was written. It provides irrefutable physical evidence that the Book of Mormon was not written by a single author but is a compilation of many contributing writers, as the prophet Joseph Smith claimed. It constitutes an absolute, tangible substantiation that the Book of Mormon is indeed a translation of an ancient history recorded on plates of gold.

The first use of the word "*or*" to correct a "slip of the stylus" in the Book of Mormon occurs when Nephi wrote the following statement;

*"Wherefore, the things which he shall write are just and true; and behold they are written in the book which thou beheld proceeding out of the mouth of the Jew, and at the time* **they** *proceeded out of the mouth of the Jew,* or, *at the time the* **book** *proceeded out of the mouth of the Jew, the things which were written were plain and pure, and most*

*precious and easy to the understanding of all men."*[97]

The subtle yet significantly revealing mistake Nephi made in this verse was in his inadvertent use of the word *"they"*. In this passage of scripture Nephi is obviously referring to the Bible. The plural word *"they"* refers to the covenants Nephi was writing about. Nephi apparently meant to refer to the book, not the covenants, that proceeded *"out of the mouth of the Jew"*. But what could he do? The lines were already inscribed into the metal. There was no delete button, no backspace, no white-out and no eraser he could use to correct his writing.

Recognizing his error, Nephi adds the corrective word *"or"* and then repeats the phrase using the word *"book"* instead of the word *"they"*.

If, as the opponents to Mormonism claim, Joseph Smith had conjured up the Book of Mormon from his own imagination, perpetuating a horrendous fraud on the world, would this young lad have thought to include such a mistake in his writings? Would he not, instead, have tried to produce a work that had no evidence of human imperfection? Taken by itself, this mistake would be

---

[97] 1 Nephi 14:23.

relatively insignificant in proving the authenticity of the Book of Mormon. There are, however, nearly 70 such mistakes in this sacred record which all attest to its authenticity.

Perhaps the most obvious example of the word *"or"* being used to correct an inadvertent mistake is found in Alma when Mormon comments;

*"And thus we see that, when these Lamanites were brought to believe and to know the truth, they were firm, and would suffer even unto death rather than commit sin, and thus we see that* **they buried their weapons of peace**,*"* [98]

Have you ever read this verse and thought, "What? They buried their weapons of *peace*? What in the world is a weapon of peace?"

Obviously, Mormon was trying to say that the Lamanites had buried their weapons of war, but as his thoughts must have rushed ahead to his upcoming statement about peace, he mistakenly scribed the word *"peace"* in place of *"war"*, accidentally claiming that the Lamanites had buried their *"weapons of peace"*.

---

[98] Alma 24:19.

Opps! Another mistake. But what could he do? As we mentioned earlier, he couldn't just crumple up the page and start over. He wouldn't want to mar the sacred writing by scratching out the word "peace". But he could correct his mistake by adding the proper phrase, *"weapons of war"*, preceded by the conjunction "*or*";

**"...<u>or</u> they buried the weapons of war, for peace."**

When Mormon abridged the history of General Moroni's first battle with the Lamanites under Zerahemnah, he explains the importance of the armor Moroni's soldiers wore. He tells us that;

*"While on the other hand, there was now and then a man fell among the Nephites, by their swords and the loss of blood, they* **being shielded from the more vital parts of the body**..." Another opps!

Unless the Lamanites were flinging vital body parts at the Nephites, Mormon undoubtedly never intended to say that the soldiers were protected by their armor from the more vital parts of the body! So he again corrects himself by adding the corrective conjunction "or";

"... <u>or</u> **the more vital parts of the body being shielded from the strokes of the Lamanites**, by their breastplates, and their arm-shields, and their head-plates." [99]

Another and more obvious form of correction used by the authors of the Book of Mormon was adding the word *"rather"* to the corrective form of the word *"or"*. In so doing, the writers remove any uncertainty that they are correcting a word or phrase that was unintentionally incorrect. There are eleven such corrections throughout the Book of Mormon.

*"And it came to pass when they had been in prison two days they were again brought before the king, and their bands were loosed, and they stood before the king, and were* **permitted** <u>or rather</u> **commanded**, *that they should answer the questions which he should ask them."* [100]

---

[99] Alma 43:38.
[100] Mosiah 7:8.

"But a seer can know of things which are past, and also of things which are to come, and by them shall **all things be revealed <u>or, rather, shall secret things be made manifest</u>**." [101]

---

"And it came to pass that they took him; and his name was Nehor, and they carried him upon the top of the hill Manti, and there he was **caused, <u>or rather</u> did acknowledge**, between the heavens and the earth that what he had taught to the people was contrary to the word of God; and there he suffered an ignominious death." [102]

---

"And thus he cleared **the ground <u>or rather</u> the bank**, which was on the west of the river Sidon, throwing the bodies of the Lamanites who had been slain into the waters of Sidon." [103]

---

[101] Mosiah 8:17.
[102] Alma 1:1-5.
[103] Alma 2:34.

"Now Ammon **being the chief among them,** <u>or rather</u> **he did administer unto them,** and he departed from them, after having blessed them according to their several stations." [104]

---

"**Now if a man desired to serve God, it was his privilege;** <u>or rather,</u> **if he believed in God it was his privilege to serve him;** but if he did not believe in him there was no law to punish him." [105]

---

"Yea, and **I had murdered many of his children** <u>or rather</u> **led them away unto destruction.**" [106]

---

[104] Alma 17:18.
[105] Alma 30:9.
[106] Alma 36:14

"And now, my son, this was the ministry unto which ye were called, to declare these glad tidings unto this people **to prepare their minds; <u>or rather</u> that salvation might come unto them, that they may prepare the minds of their children** to hear the word at the time of his coming." [107]

---

"Now behold, **the people who were in the land Bountiful <u>or rather</u> Moroni** feared that they would hearken to the words of Morianton and unite with his people." [108]

---

"And now behold, I have somewhat to say concerning the people of Ammon, who in the beginning, were Lamanites; but **by Ammon and his brethren <u>or rather</u> by the power and word of God**, they had been converted unto the Lord." [109]

---

[107] Alma 39:16.
[108] Alma 50:32.
[109] Alma 53:10.

"Behold, Ammoron, I have written unto you somewhat concerning this war **which ye have waged against my people,** <u>or rather</u> **which thy brother hath waged against them** and which ye are still determined to carry on after his death." [110]

---

The Book of Mormon authors thought that certain mistakes may have required an amplified phrase to correct the error. In five separate verses the writers expanded their corrections as follows;

---

"For the things which some men esteem to be of great worth, both to the body and soul, others set at naught and trample under their feet. Yea, even the very God of Israel do men trample under their feet; <u>I say trample under their feet but I would speak in other words</u>—they set him at naught, and hearken not to the voice of his counsels." [111]

---

[110] Alma 54:5.
[111] 1 Nephi 19:7.

"And now behold, we have come, and been forth amongst them; and we have been patient in our sufferings, and we have suffered every privation; yea, we have traveled from house to house, relying upon the mercies of the world—<u>not upon the mercies of the world alone but upon the mercies of God</u>." [112]

---

"<u>Behold, I said that the city of Ammonihah had been rebuilt. I say unto you, yea, that it was in part rebuilt</u>." [113]

---

"And behold, in the end of this book ye shall see that this Gadianton did prove the overthrow, yea, almost the entire destruction of the people of Nephi. <u>Behold I do not mean the end of the book of Helaman, but I mean the end of the book of Nephi</u>, from which I have taken all the account which I have written." [114]

---

[112] Alma 26:28.
[113] Alma 49:3.
[114] Helaman 2:13, 14.

> "And in the fifty and first year of the reign of the judges there was peace also, save it were the pride which began to enter into the church—<u>not into the church of God, but into the hearts of the people who professed to belong to the church of God.</u>" [115]

---

Additional proof of the authenticity of the Book of Mormon is found in the relative distribution of the "*or*" corrections in the Book of Mormon. The consistency with the particular circumstances of each of the various authors demonstrates a subtle yet significant confirmation of the authenticity of the writings when we examine the number of verses per error written by each author, or in each segment of the book.

When we examine the rate of mistakes made by first-person authors against those made by writers who were abridging the works of others, we find that the frequency of mistakes is higher in the abridgements than in the original compositions. There are 2.2 fewer errors in the first person accounts.

---

[115] Helaman 3:33.

Examining the frequency of errors between the Small Plates of Nephi and Mormon's abridgement of the Large Plates shows an error rate 5.4 times greater in the abridgement. In the Small Plates an error occurs only once in every 319 verses but in the Large Plates an error occurs once in every 59 verses. This statistically significant difference in the first person accounts clearly demonstrates that these two separate sections were written by at least two distinct authors.

Another significant contrast exists in the variance between the number of mistakes Mormon made compared to the number of mistakes of his son, Moroni. Mormon's error rate is over ten times higher than that of Moroni.

Most of Mormon's life was spent on the battlefield. He was chosen to direct the Nephite army when he was only 16 years old. He led his soldiers until he was 52. Between the ages of 52 and 65 he renounced his command because of the wickedness of the people. Then, at age 65 he again took up the sword and remained in battle until he was killed at age 74.

In contrast, Moroni spent most of his life alone and in hiding. He was a fugitive from the

Lamanites and the lone survivor of the Nephite nation for over 20 years.

Mormon's account, written on the run as it were, contains significantly more mistakes than Moroni's, who had plenty of time to focus and concentrate on the demanding task of accurately preparing the sacred writings. Moroni incurred only one mistake in 572 verses. That is the lowest error rate of all the Book of Mormon authors. His remarkable exactness is uniform with his unique position of 20 plus years of solitude during which time he recorded his sacred writings.

Having plenty of time to review the revered records, Moroni would certainly have been aware of the method the previous authors of the Book of Mormon used to correct their writings. He undoubtedly read through the plates many times during the 20 years he spent alone. His poignant statement, *"Behold, we know no fault"*, may very well refer to the fact that all of the "slips of the stylus" had been corrected in the manner unique to the Book of Mormon authors.

The appearance of the *"or"* corrections in the Book of Mormon translation by Joseph Smith affirms the literality of his translation and supports his claim that the Book of Mormon is a compilation of writing made by numerous authors over an extended period.

# Breakdown of Error Correction Frequency[116]

| Source | Verses | Corrections | Verses per Correction |
|---|---|---|---|
| Small plates | 1598 | 5 | 319 |
| Large Plates | 4476 | 76 | 59 |
| **1st Person Writings** | | | |
| Nephi | 918 | 3 | 306 |
| Jacob | 266 | 0 | - |
| Jarom | 14 | 1 | 14 |
| Mormon [1] | 412 | 5 | 82 |
| Moroni [2] | 216 | 0 | - |
| TOTAL | 1826 | 8 | 228 |
| **Abridgement** | | | |
| Mormon [3] | 3902 | 71 | 55 |
| Moroni [3] | 354 | 1 | 354 |
| TOTAL | 4256 | 72 | 59 |
| Total – Mormon | 4314 | 76 | 57 |
| Total – Moroni | 570 | 1 | 570 |

[1] Includes The Words of Mormon and 141 verses of commentary in the Large Plates.
[2] Includes 79 verses of commentary in The Book of Ether.
[3] Includes abridged verses and direct quotations in the abridgement.

---

[116] The Breakdown of Error Correction Frequency Table and reference material were developed and provided by Book of Mormon scholar H. Clay Gorton. It is used here with his express consent and permission.

# References to the Corrective *"OR"*

1 Ne. 14:23 19:4 19:7**

Jacob 5:21

Jarorm 1:14

Mos. 2:31 5:2 7:1, 8* 15, 18 8:17* 11:18 18:4 22:6 25:2 26:39 29:41

Alma 1:15* 2:34* 4:19 5:25 9:1 10:13, 14 11:1, 46 12:1, 31 13:16 14:11 16:16 17:14, 18*(2), 29 19:14,19 21:20 22:19 23:6 24:15, 19 26:28** 30:9* 34:13 35:15 36:14* 37:21 39:16* 43:16, 19, 38, 44 44:23 45:13 46:10 47:2 49:2-3** 50:32* 51:6 53:3, 10* 54:3,5*, 6 56:14, 18 57:8 58:20 59:3 61:8 63:15

Hel 2:13-14** 3:33** 4:22 10:17 11:24 14:21, 31

3 Ne. 3:14 12:23

Morm. 2:1 5:14

Ether 11:21

Moro. 8:22, 27

*— "or rather"

**— amplified explanation

## The Message in the Mistakes

The obvious message in the corrections found scattered throughout the Book of Mormon is that Joseph Smith did not write the Book of Mormon but served, as he constantly claimed throughout his life, as the translator of an ancient text.

Would Joseph Smith have thought to include 70 imperfections in this inspired work?

No. If Joseph were perpetuating a fraud on his followers and the world at large, he would have made this falsehood as flawless and authentic as possible.

Would Joseph Smith have thought up the idea that the prophet scribes of old might have slipped up in their writing now and again?

Not very likely. Even Moroni tells us that he knows of no fault in his work. This is because every fault or imperfection the original authors made was corrected by them using the conjunctive word "or". Therefore, no fault remained.

Would Joseph Smith have invented the unique and distinctive method of correcting the faults by employing the conjunctive "or" followed by a re-write of the original and intended thought?

What are the chances that a young man with no more than a third-grade education could write over 500 pages of text, include dozens of Hebrew literary forms such as chiasmus, and then, on top of all that, invent a procedure for correcting imperfections in the original writing? Such a thing would never have been thought of.

Would Joseph Smith have then had the foresight to vary the ratio of corrections based on the differing circumstances of Nephi, Mormon, Moroni and others?

Consider the fact that after translating the Book of Mormon, Joseph spent the remainder of his life testifying of its truthfulness often amid harsh criticism. Never once did he allude to these hidden faults as evidence of the truthfulness of the Book of Mormon. Consider also that, if he had interwoven such a fantastic fraud in his writings and in the face of such overwhelming opposition to his claims, would he have purposefully carried that secret of his deception to the grave, hoping that someone, some 150 years or so in the future, would discover his little secret and share it with the world?

The answer is a resounding no! The obvious message of these corrections testify that the Book of Mormon was indeed an ancient compilation of historic writings delivered to Joseph Smith by the angel Moroni and translated by the gift and power of God. No other explanation could account for the corrections carried within its pages.

The Prophet Joseph Smith is one of the most charismatic and influential religious figures in American history. The testimony of the prophet Joseph Smith about the Savior Jesus Christ and about the Book of Mormon should be seriously and prayerfully considered by all who want to receive a testimony of the its truths revealed from God.

I invite anyone to come and learn more about the Prophet Joseph Smith. If you will do so with an open heart and an open mind, having a true desire to know the truth, you will be able to find answers to your questions.

*"We have in the Book of Mormon an ancient Semitic treasure—a masterpiece of literary style that has yet to reach its zenith in appreciation and acclaim."* [117]

---

[117] Crowell, Angela. "Hebrew Poetry in the Book of Mormon," *The Zarahemla Record* (1986).

## The Only Absolute Proof

There is ample and abundant evidence that the Book of Mormon is true. But all of the archeological, scientific or literary evidence in the world could never convey a stronger conviction to the truth of this sacred book than the pure and undeniable witness of the Holy Spirit.

The Lord has promised us a more sure witness of the truth. This more sure witness is the witness of the Holy Ghost. John explains that;

*"It is the Spirit that beareth witness, because the Spirit is truth."* [118]

Paul declares that;

---

[118] 1 John5:6.

"No man knoweth of the things of God except by the Spirit of God." [119]

The best way to discover the truth of spiritual and religious teachings is to ask God. Jesus Christ Himself admonishes us to;

"*Ask, and it shall be given you.*" [120]

And James further counsels us;

"*Let him ask in faith, nothing wavering.*" [121]

Ezra Taft Benson asserted that;

"*We are not required to prove that the Book of Mormon is true or is an authentic record through external evidences—though there are many....God has built in his own proof system of the Book of Mormon as found in Moroni.*" [122]

Moroni proposed a specific procedure for obtaining a knowledge of the truth of spiritual

---

[119] 1 Corinthians 2:11.
[120] Matthew 7:7.
[121] James 1:6.
[122] Benson, Ezra Taft, A Witness and a Warning, Deseret Book, Salt Lake City, Utah, 1988, p. 31.

things. This would include the knowledge that the Book of Mormon is true.

*"Behold, I would exhort you that when ye shall read these things, if it be wisdom in God that ye should read them, that ye would remember how merciful the Lord hath been unto the children of men, from the creation of Adam even down until the time that ye shall receive these things, and ponder it in your hearts.*

*"And when ye shall receive these things, I would exhort you that ye would ask God, the Eternal Father, in the name of Christ, if these things are not true; and if ye shall ask with a sincere heart, with real intent, having faith in Christ, he will manifest the truth of it unto you, by the power of the Holy Ghost.*

*"And by the power of the Holy Ghost ye may know the truth of all things."* [123]

We have been given ample witnesses in our day that the work of this dispensation is true. We have the testimony of holy prophets. God has sent angels again to the earth. He has provided human witnesses to His holy work. Further, He has

---

[123] Moroni 10:3-5.

promised us a personal witness through the Holy Spirit if we are sincere and faithful.

The scriptures also teach that...

*"...signs shall follow them that believe."* [124]

The Lord is willing to show us signs. He is willing to prove all His works. But any physical sign, evidence, or proof will have no real meaning or value if we have no true faith. Faith precedes signs. Signs are given to develop faith which already exists and they are never intended to replace faith. If we are interested in proving that the Book of Mormon is true, we need to seek for faith rather than seeking for signs.

This is perhaps one reason why the gold plates, the Urim and Thummim and the breastplate discovered by Joseph Smith are not on display. The Lord told Joseph;

*"I have reserved those things which I have entrusted unto you, my servant Joseph, for a wise purpose in me, and it shall be made known unto*

---

[124] Mark 16:17.

*future generations; but this generation shall have my word through you."* [125]

To the rest of us He said;

*"Ye receive no witness until after the trial of your faith."* [126]

You can, however, find and accept evidence and proof of the authenticity of the Book of Mormon through the following process;

1. You must *desire* to know that the Book of Mormon is true. You need to hold a sincere desire for truth. The desire to know must be a firm, constant, and burning desire, otherwise, you will not pay the price required to gain a sure testimony. A true witness comes only to those who desire it.
2. You must *read and ponder* the teachings of the Book of Mormon. Isn't it ironic that we devote so much time to developing job skills or furthering our earthly education; yet we think we can understand the gospel of Jesus Christ with a few passing glances at the scriptures? The gospel should be studied

---
[125] D&C 5:9, 10.
[126] Ether 12:6.

more intently than any other subject. Study the Book of Mormon. Know the message it contains.

3. You must *ask* God whether or not the Book of Mormon is true. Our Father in heaven knows if the Book of Mormon is all that it claims to be. What greater witness can you have?

The degree to which we are willing to accept any evidence of the truthfulness of the Book of Mormon will be determined by how devoted we are to adhering to these three simple steps.

Revelation is the key to knowledge. You can **know.** You do not need to remain in doubt. Follow the preceding prescribed procedure and you can have an absolute assurance that the Book of Mormon is the word of God. God will make it known to you when you surrender yourself to the promptings of the Holy Spirit and are ready to learn.

A firm and abiding witness of the Book of Mormon is not reserved exclusively for the prophets, apostles or leaders in the church. A witness of the truth is a free gift from God to anyone willing to go through the process of building their own testimony.

*"Anyone can acquire this testimony by following the established procedure by which the*

*Lord gives a testimony. There are no shortcuts. A desire to know is imperative. To learn the doctrine is essential. To do his will will sanctify that teaching in your heart. To pray often will open the way and make all things possible through him, for he has said, '...without me ye can do nothing.'"* [127]

The power of the Book of Mormon will fill your life as you begin a serious study of its sacred message. As you hunger and thirst after *"the words of life"* [128] you will discover life in greater abundance. I entreat you with all sincerity to consider with solemnity the purpose and importance of the Book of Mormon.

As the prophet Joseph attests, the Book of Mormon is the keystone of our religion and we can *"get nearer to God by abiding by its precepts than by any other book."* It is my sincere prayer and desire that the Book of Mormon become, not only the keystone of your religion, but also the keystone of your life.

---

[127] Simpson, Robert L., New Era, Mar. 1972, pp. 4, 6. Also, John 15:5.
[128] D&C 84:85.

# A Free Offer

The Book of Mormon is another witness of Jesus Christ which supports and confirms the truths found in the Bible and in its testimony of the Savior. A verse from the Book of Mormon declares that it...

*"...shall establish the truth"* of the Bible and *"shall make known to all kindreds, tongues, and people, that the Lamb of God is the Son of the Eternal Father, and the savior of the world; and all men must come unto him, or they cannot be saved."* [129]

Both the Book of Mormon and the Bible are a collection of doctrines and instructions recorded by early prophets. The Bible describes incidents in and around the Middle East while the Book of Mormon

---

[129] 1 Nephi 13:40.

documents the lives of the occupants of ancient America from approximately 600 BC to 400 AD.

The Book of Mormon, like the Bible, was written and compiled over time by various ancient prophets who held the spirit of prophecy and revelation. Their words were quoted and abridged by Mormon and explain the doctrines of the gospel, the plan of salvation, and the steps we must follow to gain eternal salvation.

Joseph Smith, Jr. translated the Book of Mormon into English by the gift and power of God. It has now been published in many different languages as an additional witness that Jesus Christ is the Son of the living God. With more than 6,000 verses, the Book of Mormon makes reference to Jesus Christ nearly 4000 times!

Everyone is invited and encouraged to read the Book of Mormon, to ponder its powerful message in their hearts and then to ask God if the book is true. If you pursue this task with faith and sincerity of heart, you will gain a testimony of its truth and divinity by the power of the Holy Ghost. [130]

*"Those who gain this divine witness from the holy Spirit will also come to know by the same power that Jesus Christ is the Savior of the world,*

---

[130] Moromi 10:3-5.

*that Joseph Smith is his revelator and prophet in these last days, and that the Church of Jesus Christ of Latter-day Saints is the Lord's kingdom once again established on the earth, preparatory to the second coming of the Messiah."* [131]

If you are interested in reading the Book of Mormon and discovering for yourself the valuable truths it contains, you may request a FREE copy of the book at the church's website:

www.mormon.org/free-book-of-mormon

Free Book of Mormon | Mormon.org

---

[131] From the Introduction of the Book of Mormon.

## About the Author

Bill Wylson, author of *Three Minutes Eighteen Seconds: A Prophet's Message to the World* and *Seven Success Strategies for Latter-day Saints* lives in Salt Lake City, Utah.

Watch for his next work, *Give Place in Your Heart: 31 Promises from the Book of Mormon* coming soon from White Horse LDS Books.

www.myldsbooks.com

White Horse LDS Books

Salt Lake City, Utah

www.ingramcontent.com/pod-product-compliance
Lightning Source LLC
Chambersburg PA
CBHW071306040426
42444CB00009B/1900